Level B

Content Reading
Social Science

Writer: Jeanette Leardi

Editor: Michelle McCardell

Cover designer: Mike Reilly

Interior designer: Adam Chlan

Illustrators: Pages 3, 6 Murray Callahan
Pages 16, 20, 38, 40, 42, 52 Margaret Sanfilippo

Photo credits: Cover: riding bikes, PhotoDisc, Inc.; Tom Thumb, © Bettman/CORBIS; Sally Ride, NASA; boys raising flag, PhotoDisc, Inc. Page 8: AP Wide World Photos/Beth Keiser. Page 10: PhotoDisc, Inc. Page 12: PhotoDisc, Inc. Page 14: National Portrait Gallery, Smithsonian Institution, gift of the Harmon Foundation. Page 18: © Mark Millmore 1997–2001. Page 22: Colin Kent, www.kenzingtonphotos.com. Page 24: © Deide von Schawen, 2000–2002 Pei Cobb Freed & Partners. Page 26: National Portrait Gallery, Smithsonian Institution, gift of an anonymous donor. Page 28: Tami Keeler, Manchester City, Vermont. Page 30: Eyewire, Inc. Page 32: courtesy of Picanol N.V., Belgium. Page 34: Adam Chlan. Page 36: NASA. Page 44: © The Independence Hall Association, www.ushistory.org. Page 46: © Russ Finley–Holiday Film Corp. Page 48: courtesy of the B&O Railroad Museum, Inc. Page 50: courtesy of the Jane Addams Hull House Association. Page 54: photo by Michael Provost, courtesy of Kaylor Management, Inc.

ISBN 978-0-8454-9271-0

Copyright © 2002 The Continental Press, Inc.

No part of this publication may be reproduced in any form or by any means, electronic, mechanical, photocopying, recording, or otherwise, without the prior written permission of the publisher. All rights reserved. Printed in the United States of America.

 **Continental Press**

Contents

Where Milk Comes From..3
Children Are Neighbors, Too..6
Our Neighbors Come from Everywhere..............................8
The Many Uses of a Library..10
How American Schools Have Changed...........................12
Mary McLeod Bethune, Teacher with a Dream..............14
Ball Games Through the Ages..16
Writing with Pictures..18
Calendars Around the World..20
Why Cities Build Skyscrapers...22
I. M. Pei, an Architect for Our Times.............................24
Why the United States Has a President........................26
The Making of the First Traffic Light.............................28
Why Money Is Important..30
How a Shirt Is Made...32
A Visit to Hershey, Pennsylvania....................................34
Sally Ride, First American Woman in Space.................36
The Important Trips of Christopher Columbus..............38
Early Explorers of the American West..........................40
How the Thanksgiving Holiday Began...........................42
Our American Flag...44
The Story of the American Buffalo................................46
The Railroad in the United States.................................48
Jane Addams, a Helper to All..50
Native American Beadwork..52
Tania León, Maker of Music...54
Glossary...56

This book is called **Content Reading**. It has stories about different times and people. After each story are some questions. They will help you remember and understand what you read.

These first three pages teach you what to do. First, read the story. Then answer the questions. Check your work each time. Read about the question and the answers. Change your answer if you need to.

Where Milk Comes From

Milk is a very important food. It has almost everything that we need to stay well. Butter, cheese, and ice cream are made from milk.

Long ago, most families owned a cow. Now many people live in cities. They can't have cows. So milk travels a long way from the <u>farm</u> to your kitchen.

Cows used to be milked by hand. Today, most cows are milked by machines. Milk leaves the farm in big trucks. It goes to factories where it is heated. Heating kills anything in the milk that might make you sick. After heating, the milk is put into bottles and boxes. Then, these are shipped to stores. Finally, people buy the milk to take home.

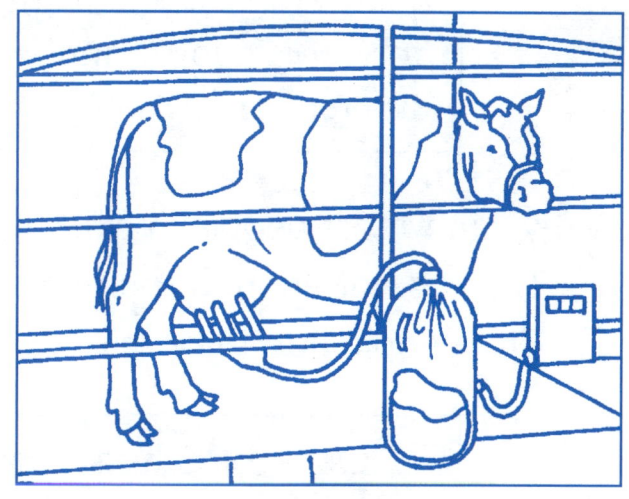

Milk can come from other animals, too. Many people drink milk from goats, sheep, and deer. Some even drink camel milk!

Social Science

Put an X in the box (☐) beside the best answer.

1. Today, most cows are milked _____.
   ☐ by hand   ☒ by machines   ☐ in factories   ☐ outside barns

   > The first question is about a **fact.** You may remember the answer. If not, look back at the story. The answer is in paragraph 3. It says, "Today, most cows are milked by machines." So your answer should be "by machines."

2. The main idea of paragraph 4 is that people drink milk _____.
   ☐ because it's good for them   ☐ less in the summer
   ☐ from cows only   ☒ from many different animals

   > This question asks about a **main idea.** The main idea is what the story or paragraph is mostly about. Here the question is about paragraph 4. Find the paragraph. Read it again quickly. Now look at the answers. The best answer is people drink milk "from many different animals."

3. Why can't most people in cities have cows?
   ☒ There is not enough room in cities.   ☐ Cows need fresh air.
   ☐ City people don't like milk.   ☐ Farmers won't sell cows.

   > Question 3 asks about **something that is not in the story.** You need to use your own ideas to decide what is probably true. Think about the question. Look at the answers. The best answer is "There is not enough room in cities."

4   Content Reading

4. What happens right **after** milk is put into bottles and boxes?
   - ☐ People buy it.
   - ☒ It is shipped to stores.
   - ☐ Farmers sell it to factories.
   - ☐ It is heated to kill bad things.

> Question 4 is about putting **steps or events in order.** Here you must decide what happens after milk is packed. Look at paragraph 3. It says, "Then, these are shipped to stores." This is the best answer.

5. In paragraph 2, the word **farm** means a place where people _____.
   - ☒ raise animals
   - ☐ make ice cream
   - ☐ buy milk
   - ☐ live close together

> This question is about a **word.** You must decide what it means. Find the word **farm** in paragraph 2. Then look at the answers. A **farm** is a place where people "raise animals."

Write your answer to this question on the lines.

Would you like your family to own a cow? Why or why not?

I dont want to cause they are smelly and the noice they make is so anoying

> The last question asks you to think about what you have read and what you already know. There is no "correct" answer. But you might need to use facts from the story. Always be sure to give reasons for your answer.

Social Science

Children Are Neighbors, Too

No matter where you live, you have neighbors. They may live right next door. Or they may live miles away.

Neighbors work together to make their community a good place to live. They make laws that keep people safe. They vote for the <u>leaders</u> of their town or city. These are things that grown-ups do. But you can help, too. You can be a good neighbor in lots of ways.

For one thing, you can follow the rules for keeping safe. You should look both ways before you cross a street. You should go up to a police officer if you are lost. You should call 911 if you are hurt or in trouble.

There are other ways to be a good neighbor. Do not throw garbage on the ground or out of a car window. Do not throw out old newspapers or bottles. Instead, you can take them to special places. There, they can be turned into new things and used again.

There is another important way you can be a good neighbor. You can work hard in school and learn all that you can. This way, you will be able to help others when you grow up.

So be a good neighbor, starting right now.

Content Reading

Put an X in the box (☐) beside the best answer.

1. Neighbors make a place good to live in by _____.
   ☐ fighting with one another
   ☐ working together
   ☐ waiting for others to help
   ☐ moving to another place

2. The main idea of this story is that children _____.
   ☐ can be good neighbors   ☐ should go to school
   ☐ do not have to follow rules   ☐ make the laws

3. You can probably say that children who follow the rules _____.
   ☐ are bad neighbors   ☐ are smart and safe
   ☐ can do anything they want   ☐ are angry

4. What should you do **before** you cross a street?
   ☐ Ask the police to help you.   ☐ Look at the ground.
   ☐ Call 911.   ☐ Look both ways.

5. In paragraph 2, the word **leaders** means people who _____.
   ☐ follow others   ☐ do not follow rules
   ☐ are in charge   ☐ live far away

• •

Write your answer to this question on the lines.

Why is it important for neighbors to follow the laws where they live?

_____

_____

_____

Social Science

Our Neighbors Come from Everywhere

You probably have neighbors from many lands. That's how our country has grown. More people come to America than to any other country. For over 300 years, people have come here to find a better life. Others come to be free to live the way they choose. Our laws help everyone live together in peace.

All of our families came here from somewhere. The Native Americans came first, from Asia. Then other people came from Europe and Africa. Still others came from Canada, Mexico, South America, and again from Asia. Look in a phone book. There are many different kinds of names.

Life can be hard for new people in the United States. It takes time to learn our language and ways of living. At first, many new Americans live near others from their old land. That way, things don't seem as strange. So our cities have many different neighborhoods. In one **block**, the people might speak Spanish. In the next block, they might speak Chinese. But their children and their children's children grow up to be Americans.

The United States is lucky. The many different people add new ideas and customs to our lives.

Put an X in the box (☐) beside the best answer.

1. It takes time for someone to learn a new _____.
   ☐ number ☐ language ☐ trick ☐ book

2. The main idea of paragraph 2 is that Americans _____.
   ☐ come from many lands   ☐ find better jobs
   ☐ have been here all the time   ☐ travel everywhere

3. Things seem strange to new people here probably because _____.
   ☐ Americans are strange
   ☐ they live in neighborhoods
   ☐ they don't like America
   ☐ our ways may be different

4. What happens **last**?
   ☐ People leave their countries.
   ☐ People come to the United States.
   ☐ People become Americans.
   ☐ People are unhappy at home.

5. In paragraph 3, the word **block** means _____.
   ☐ a hard piece   ☐ to be in the way of
   ☐ a street   ☐ to keep from

• •

Write your answer to this question on the lines.

What kinds of things do you think you can learn from your neighbors?

_____

_____

_____

Social Science

The Many Uses of a Library

A library is a place where many books are kept. You can read a book there. Or, you can <u>borrow</u> it and return it when you are done. In a library, you can also find magazines, CDs, and tapes.

Libraries have computers. You can find out about books and other things. With a home computer, you can visit the library without leaving your house. Or you can borrow books and tapes from a special bus or van. It takes things from the library to different parts of town.

Now, to do all of these things, you need a library card. With that card, you can borrow things or look them up on your computer. To get a library card, ask a grown-up to take you to your library. The librarian there will help you.

Other special things happen at the library. Most libraries have story time. That is when someone reads a book or tells a story to children. Libraries are also places where people hold meetings. And a library may have special places to show works of art.

A library is a very special part of your community. Visit it as often as you can. You will learn a lot there. And you will have fun doing it.

Put an X in the box (☐) beside the best answer.

1. People go to a library to take home _____.
   ☐ money   ☐ toys
   ☐ tools   ☐ books

2. The main idea of this story is that a library _____.
   ☐ has books to read   ☐ helps people in lots of ways
   ☐ has computers in it   ☐ has a story time

3. You can decide from the story that people who use libraries _____.
   ☐ are silly   ☐ get tired
   ☐ learn a lot   ☐ need money

4. What happens **after** you get a library card?
   ☐ You don't have to learn anymore.
   ☐ You will know how to read.
   ☐ You can take home books.
   ☐ You can go to school.

5. In paragraph 1, the word **borrow** means _____.
   ☐ use for a while, then return   ☐ keep as long as you want
   ☐ own for the rest of your life   ☐ give away to someone

• •

Write your answer to this question on the lines.

Why do you think it is important for a city or town to have a library?

_____

_____

_____

_____

Social Science

How American Schools Have Changed

Today, you go to school to learn many things. But 300 years ago, children in America learned things in a different way.

Long ago, people who came to America had a very hard life. Children helped their parents farm the land. They did not go to school. Instead, their parents <u>taught</u> them at home. The children learned how to read and write. But they also learned how to cook and use tools. They learned how to hunt and grow food.

Later, as towns and cities grew, children went to school. At first, only rich people could send their children to school. Often, the school was one room with just one teacher. Children of all ages learned together. The teacher taught different lessons to different children.

For a long time, only white children could go to school. But after the Civil War, African American children started going to school. Many years later, all children began going to the same schools.

Today, you and your friends learn things that early American children never dreamed of. You learn about space travel. You learn to use a computer. You take trips with your class to museums and zoos.

Content Reading

Put an X in the box (☐) beside the best answer.

1. Long ago, children in America learned _____.
   ☐ how to use a computer
   ☐ about space travel
   ☐ in schools with many rooms
   ☐ how to cook and use tools

2. The main idea of this story is that American schools _____.
   ☐ teach many things
   ☐ have changed a lot over time
   ☐ were once very large
   ☐ have always been the same

3. Only rich children used to go to school probably because _____.
   ☐ they could read
   ☐ poor children had to work
   ☐ they wanted to learn
   ☐ teachers liked them

4. What happened **after** the Civil War?
   ☐ African American children could not go to school.
   ☐ White children no longer had to go to school.
   ☐ All schools had more than one room.
   ☐ African American children started going to school.

5. In paragraph 2, the word **taught** means _____.
   ☐ helped a person learn
   ☐ went to
   ☐ pulled tight
   ☐ made something

• •

Write your answer to this question on the lines.

What are some things you know that children in early America did not learn about?

_____

_____

_____

Social Science

Mary McLeod Bethune, Teacher with a Dream

Mary McLeod was an African American. She was born in 1875. Her parents were slaves who were later freed. Mary's parents wanted their children to have an <u>education</u>. But at the time, hardly any African Americans went to school. And none of them went to schools for white children.

When Mary was 11, she was finally able to go to school. It was a new school for African American children. Mary worked hard and was a good student. Later, she went to a school in Chicago. Mary was the only African American in the whole school.

Mary knew that she wanted to be a teacher. She wanted to help other African Americans. In 1898, Mary married Albertus Bethune. A year later, they moved to Florida, and Mary got her wish. She built a school in Daytona, Florida, for African American girls.

In 1904, the school opened. There were five girl students. At first, the school had no tables and chairs. So Mary made them from boxes. As the years passed, the school grew to 14 buildings and 400 students. Today, it is a college, and African American boys go there, too.

Content Reading

Put an X in the box (☐) beside the best answer.

1. Mary McLeod Bethune started a school for _____.
   ☐ white girls   ☐ rich people
   ☐ parents   ☐ African American girls ✓

2. The main idea of paragraph 2 is that Mary _____.
   ☐ was a good student ✓   ☐ did not like school
   ☐ went to Florida   ☐ got married

3. When Mary was little, she did not have white friends probably because _____.
   ☐ she did not want any   ☐ they were older
   ☐ they could not go to school together   ☐ Mary was shy

4. What did Mary do **before** opening her school?
   ☐ moved to Chicago   ☐ got married
   ☐ made tables and chairs   ☐ opened a college

5. In paragraph 1, the word <u>education</u> means _____.
   ☐ good job   ☐ big house
   ☐ money   ☐ learning

• •

Write your answer to this question on the lines.

Why do you think Mary McLeod Bethune was able to make her wish come true?

_____

_____

_____

_____

Social Science 15

Ball Games Through the Ages

Ball games go a long way back in time. The first balls were probably stones.

In <u>ancient</u> Egypt, people played a special game. Someone would hit a cloth ball with a bat. Two other people would then try to catch the ball. At parties, Greek girls often did a special dance. While they danced, they tossed a ball. It was made of hair and string. It was a kind of show for the people at the party.

Greek boys and men played a game that looked like today's soccer. The ancient Romans learned this game from the Greeks. The Romans spread soccer through the world. That is how we know the game today.

Native Americans played ball games, too. Some of them used a ball made of animal hide. They would throw the ball. Then, they would catch it using sticks with small nets at one end. Other Native Americans used sticks to push a ball on the ground. They tried to get the ball past the other team.

The ancient people of Mexico were the first to use rubber balls. Rubber came from some trees that grew there. Since rubber bounces, their game was different. It was a game like our basketball.

Put an X in the box (☐) beside the best answer.

1. The first balls were made of _____.
   ☐ rubber ☐ stone
   ☐ cloth   ☐ wood

2. The main idea of this story is that ball games _____.
   ☐ are not fun   ☐ began in Egypt
   ☐ have been around a long time ☐ were spread by the Romans

3. You can decide from the story that a basketball has to _____.
   ☐ be heavy   ☐ be big
   ☐ be Mayan   ☐ bounce

4. What happened **after** the Greeks thought up soccer?
   ☐ They taught it to the Egyptians.
   ☐ They thought up basketball.
   ☐ The Romans learned it.
   ☐ They used rubber balls.

5. In paragraph 2, the word **ancient** means _____.
   ☐ very old   ☐ not well
   ☐ very young ☐ far away

• •

Write your answer to this question on the lines.

Why didn't people around the world use the same kind of ball?

_____

_____

_____

_____

Social Science

Writing with Pictures

You write a sentence with words. But thousands of years ago, people in Egypt wrote with pictures. These pictures are called hieroglyphs (HEYE•ruh•glifs).

To write about a bird or a drum or water, Egyptians drew pictures. Later on, Egyptians used those pictures to stand for something else, too. The bird might stand not only for a bird, but also for flying. The drum might stand for music of any kind. The water might stand for a river.

Today, our words are made up of letters of the alphabet. And each letter stands for a sound. As the years went on, Egyptian hieroglyphs began to stand for sounds, too. The bird might stand for the sound of the letter A.

Then, people stopped using hieroglyphs. For many years, no one understood them. They were a mystery—even to Egyptians. But, in 1799, a big stone was found in Egypt. On this stone were lots of hieroglyphs. And right next to them were two other languages. One language was another kind of Egyptian. The other language was Greek. The same message was written out in three languages. At that time, people could read the other two languages. So they were able to understand the Egyptian pictures for the first time.

Content Reading

Put an X in the box (☐) beside the best answer.

1. Thousands of years ago, Egyptians used to write with _____.
   ☐ pens
   ☐ pictures
   ☐ words
   ☐ letters

2. The main idea of paragraph 2 is that Egyptian writing _____.
   ☐ has not changed
   ☐ changed over the years
   ☐ is easy to understand
   ☐ can only stand for one thing at a time

3. You can decide from paragraph 4 that the big stone _____.
   ☐ was an important thing to find
   ☐ was no help at all
   ☐ helped people to learn Greek
   ☐ still puzzles everyone

4. What happened **after** the big stone was found?
   ☐ People learned how to write.
   ☐ Egyptian was forgotten.
   ☐ People could read the hieroglyphs.
   ☐ No one wrote Egyptian.

5. In paragraph 4, the word **mystery** means something that is _____.
   ☐ funny
   ☐ spoken
   ☐ difficult
   ☐ not known

• •

Write your answer to this question on the lines.

What do you think might have happened if the big stone had never been found?

_____

_____

_____

Social Science

Calendars Around the World

A calendar is a way to measure time. Long ago, people looked up at the night sky. They **noticed** that the shape of the moon changed. They noticed that the stars appeared in different places. The people also noticed changes in the weather. They saw that there were seasons.

People in many lands wanted to keep track of these changes. That way, they could be ready for winter. They could also know when to plant crops. People made calendars to tell them the right times to do these things. Soon, there were calendars all over the world. But each one was different.

The Aztecs of Mexico used a stone calendar. It was big and round. A year on this calendar had 260 days. Special days were marked. On those days, people built houses or planted crops. On other special days, they went to war.

In China, people also watched the moon. The Chinese year has 12 months. But sometimes, a year has 353 days. Other times, the Chinese add a whole month. That is a leap year. A leap year can have as many as 385 days.

Today, our calendar has 12 months, with 365 days. But once every four years, we have a leap year, too. In that year, we add a whole day, February 29.

Content Reading

Put an X in the box (☐) beside the best answer.

1. Calendars measure _____.
   ☐ weather			☐ time
   ☐ the stars			☐ crops

2. The main idea of this story is that calendars _____.
   ☐ can be different		☐ must be big and round
   ☐ have always been the same	☐ have 365 days

3. You can probably decide from the story that in a leap year we have _____.
   ☐ 385 days			☐ 353 days
   ☐ 365 days			☐ 366 days

4. What happened **before** the Chinese made their calendar?
   ☐ They asked the Aztecs for help.
   ☐ They used the Aztec calendar.
   ☐ They noticed the moon.
   ☐ Their year had 365 days.

5. In paragraph 1, the word **noticed** means _____.
   ☐ saw   ☐ forgot   ☐ planned   ☐ hoped

• •

Write your answer to this question on the lines.

Why is it important for everyone to have a calendar?

_____

_____

_____

_____

Social Science

Why Cities Build Skyscrapers

Many years ago, there was plenty of land. But there were not many people. People built their homes low and spread out. Then, they began building houses closer together. This was the beginning of cities.

In the city, people could buy and sell things. They could find jobs, too. Then, about 100 years ago, cities started to become crowded. So people started to make buildings. The buildings were tall and close together instead of low and spread out.

The tallest buildings are called skyscrapers. Think of small children playing with blocks. When they spread blocks on the floor, they use a lot of space. But when they stack them, the blocks use less room on the floor. Skyscrapers are the same way. They don't use much land. And many people can live and work in each skyscraper.

Building a skyscraper is a big job. First, someone plans and draws the building. Someone else makes sure the plan is safe. Then the building begins.

Strong metal posts are set deep in the ground. These keep the building standing for a long time. Workers **connect** the posts to other metal poles. The skyscraper gets higher and higher. Soon it will have walls, windows, and doors. Not long after that, people will finally move in.

22 Content Reading

Put an X in the box (☐) beside the best answer.

1. Skyscrapers are built with metal _____.
   ☐ blocks   ☐ doors   ☐ posts   ☐ windows

2. The main idea of paragraph 3 is that skyscrapers _____.
   ☐ don't need much land   ☐ are built in cities
   ☐ are larger than houses   ☐ can be built quickly

3. In places where there is a lot of land, people probably live in _____.
   ☐ skyscrapers   ☐ low buildings
   ☐ tall buildings   ☐ barns

4. What happens **first** when a skyscraper is built?
   ☐ People move in.
   ☐ Posts are put deep in the ground.
   ☐ Posts are connected to metal poles.
   ☐ Walls and windows are added.

5. In paragraph 5, the word **connect** means _____.
   ☐ take apart   ☐ cover
   ☐ belong   ☐ join together

• •

Write your answer to this question on the lines.

How would living in a skyscraper be different from living in a house in the country?

_____

_____

_____

_____

Social Science

I. M. Pei, an Architect for Our Times

Ieoh Ming Pei (YEO MING PAY) was born in China in 1917. When he was 18 years old, he came to the United States. He wanted to be an architect and build buildings.

Pei finished school in 1940. He wanted to return to China to work. But China was at war. So Pei stayed in the United States. He began teaching at Harvard University. Then, he worked for a company as an architect. In 1955, Pei started his own company.

Pei is <u>famous</u> all over the world for his buildings. Three of them are really well known. One is the John F. Kennedy Library in Boston, Massachusetts. President Kennedy's important papers are kept there.

Another famous building is part of the Louvre Museum in Paris, France. It is in the shape of a glass pyramid. When it was built, many people thought it was very strange.

A third famous building is the Rock and Roll Hall of Fame, in Cleveland, Ohio. It has things once owned by well-known rock and roll stars.

Pei has won many prizes for his work. In 1986, President Ronald Reagan gave him the Medal of Liberty. And in 1990, President George Bush gave him the Medal of Freedom. They were a way of saying "thank you" for all his work.

Content Reading

Put an X in the box (☐) beside the best answer.

1. I. M. Pei was born in _____.
   ☐ the United States ☐ Japan
   ☐ China ☐ France

2. The main idea of the last paragraph is that Pei _____.
   ☐ has won many prizes ☐ met the presidents
   ☐ won a prize in 1986 ☐ worked around the world

3. Pei did not go back to China in 1940 probably because _____.
   ☐ there was no work for him ☐ there was a war going on
   ☐ he wanted to finish school ☐ he wasn't an architect yet

4. What did Pei do **after** he became a teacher?
   ☐ He built the Kennedy Library. ☐ He won lots of prizes.
   ☐ He started his own company. ☐ He worked for a company.

5. In paragraph 3, the word **famous** means _____.
   ☐ very well known
   ☐ nice to look at
   ☐ not very well known
   ☐ hard to build

• •

Write your answer to this question on the lines.

What do you think is the most beautiful building in your community? Tell why you think so.

_____

_____

_____

Social Science

Why the United States Has a President

Before the United States could become a country, we had to fight England. The war lasted from 1775 to 1783. George Washington led our army. Americans felt safe with him in charge. They looked up to him.

When the war was over, the United States needed a new <u>ruler</u>. Some Americans thought we should have a king, just like in England. So they asked George Washington to be the new king.

But many other Americans did not want a king. Often, a king alone decided on the laws of the land. That was too much power for one person.

So these Americans put together a plan. The people would choose their ruler every four years. This way, no one could lead for any longer than the people wanted him to.

George Washington liked this new plan. He thought it was fair for the American people. So he said "no" to being a king. But he said "yes" when Americans asked him to be our first president.

Since then, the United States has had a president, not a king. And many other countries have followed this same plan.

Content Reading

Put an X in the box (☐) beside the best answer.

1. In 1775, the United States was at war with _____.
   ☐ France   ☐ Spain   ☐ Mexico   ☐ England

2. The main idea of paragraph 3 is that some Americans _____.
   ☐ wanted a different kind of leader
   ☐ wanted George Washington to be king
   ☐ did not want to have a president
   ☐ still liked England's king

3. You can decide from the story that every four years, Americans _____.
   ☐ decide if there should be a war   ☐ choose a king
   ☐ choose a president   ☐ go to England

4. What happened **last** to George Washington?
   ☐ He was asked to be king.   ☐ He became president.
   ☐ He said "no" to being king.   ☐ He led our army.

5. In paragraph 2, the word **ruler** means _____.
   ☐ person in charge   ☐ measuring tool
   ☐ army   ☐ plan

• •

Write your answer to this question on the lines.

Would you like to be president of the United States? Why or why not?

_____

_____

_____

Social Science

The Making of the First Traffic Light

Picture a busy street corner. Here come cars and buses. There go trucks and taxis. Here come people on bikes and people crossing the street. What would happen without <u>traffic</u> rules? Watch out!

For a long time, not many traffic rules were needed. People traveled on dirt roads. They used horses to get around. Then cars were invented in the early 1900s. People could travel faster and farther. Traffic rules became more important. Drivers needed to know when to go and when to stop.

One day, Garrett Morgan saw an accident. A car crashed into a horse and wagon. Some people in the wagon were hurt. The horse later died. Garrett wanted to stop things like this from happening. So he came up with a great idea. He invented a traffic light.

The first traffic lights went up in Detroit, Michigan, in the 1920s. They worked just as ours do today. They had the same three colors. A green light told drivers to go. A red light told them to stop. And a yellow light meant slow down and get ready to stop.

People did what each colored light told them to do. Because of this, there were fewer accidents. Thanks to Garrett Morgan, traffic lights help us travel more safely.

Content Reading

Put an X in the box (☐) beside the best answer.

1. Traffic lights tell drivers when to _____.
   - ☐ drive faster
   - ☐ pass
   - ☐ walk
   - ☐ go and stop

2. The main idea of this story is that traffic lights _____.
   - ☐ make it hard for people to travel
   - ☐ were easy to invent
   - ☐ help people travel safely
   - ☐ can come in any color

3. You can decide from the story that more cars mean _____.
   - ☐ more traffic
   - ☐ fewer traffic signs
   - ☐ smaller cities
   - ☐ better roads

4. What happened **after** cars were invented?
   - ☐ Traffic rules were more important.
   - ☐ More people traveled by horse.
   - ☐ People traveled slowly.
   - ☐ Wagons were invented.

5. In paragraph 1, the word **traffic** means _____.
   - ☐ the lights at street corners
   - ☐ many cars moving along the same road
   - ☐ to drive a car
   - ☐ to travel somewhere in a car

• •

Write your answer to this question on the lines.

What is something else that was invented to make our lives safer? How does it make our lives safer?

_____

_____

_____

Social Science

Why Money Is Important

Sometimes you go to the store. You want to buy a toy. You have to pay something for your toy. What you pay has the same value as what you buy. That is the fair way of doing things.

Long ago, people would trade things they had for other things they wanted. But sometimes their goods were hard to carry. So, people got the idea to use one thing that everyone agreed was important. That was how money got started.

Money is what people get for their work. Money is what people use to pay for things they buy. So money can be almost anything. People just have to agree on it.

Long ago, people around the world used different things as money. They used beads, blankets, animals, salt, and shells.

Later, people used bars of gold and silver as money. But they were too heavy to carry around. So people began using paper and small coins. They were small enough to put in a pocket. And they lasted a long time. We still use paper and coins today.

There are special laws around the world. They tell what can be used as money. Countries make sure that people follow the laws. They keep people's money safe. That is how your money has value. That is why the money you spend is worth something. Because of this, it is safe to use.

Put an X in the box (☐) beside the best answer.

1. People began to use money when _____.
   ☐ they found out about gold and silver ☐ they ran out of shells
   ☐ it got harder to carry things to trade ☐ countries made laws

2. The main idea of this story is that money _____.
   ☐ buys everything   ☐ is not worth much
   ☐ is gold and silver   ☐ can be many things

3. Today we don't use sacks of salt for money probably because they _____.
   ☐ are not worth anything   ☐ do not last
   ☐ are easy to use   ☐ are easy to carry

4. What happened **after** people used gold for money?
   ☐ They decided it was not worth much.
   ☐ They used paper and coins.
   ☐ They used beads.
   ☐ They traded it for blankets.

5. In paragraph 1, the word <u>value</u> means what _____.
   ☐ you learn at school   ☐ somebody wants
   ☐ you put in the bank   ☐ something is worth

• •

Write your answer to this question on the lines.

Why is it important for countries to make laws about what can be used as money?

_____

_____

_____

Social Science 31

How a Shirt Is Made

Shirts are made from different things. Some are made of cotton. Others are made of wool.

Some shirts start out as a cotton plant. Cotton grows in many parts of the world. China, the United States, and India grow the most. Cotton plants are big and green. Small white balls of cotton grow on them. First, the cotton is picked. The seeds and leaves are taken out. Next, the cotton is pressed. Then it goes to a factory.

At the factory, people use machines to stretch the cotton. They spin it into thread. The thread can be white. Or, it can be made into a color. Next, other machines weave the thread into cloth. Finally, people use more machines to cut and <u>sew</u> the cloth. They make shirts from the cloth.

Shirts may also begin as sheep's wool. Scotland, Australia, and New Zealand raise lots of sheep for wool. Wool on a sheep is like hair on people. In warm weather, the wool is cut off the sheep. The wool is washed. Then it is sent to a factory. There, the wool is made into warm, heavy cloth.

Making shirts and other clothes gives many people jobs. There are farmers, truck drivers, and factory workers. There are people who sell clothes. And there are people who think of new ways for clothes to look.

Put an X in the box (☐) beside the best answer.

1. Some shirts may be made from wool or _____.
   ☐ cotton ☐ white balls
   ☐ hair ☐ oil

2. The main idea of this story is to tell about how _____.
   ☐ most cotton grows ☐ cloth is cleaned
   ☐ some shirts are made ☐ people choose clothes

3. In winter, people probably wear clothes made from _____.
   ☐ cotton ☐ wool
   ☐ machines ☐ leaves

4. What happens **before** wool is sent to a factory?
   ☐ It is spun into thread.
   ☐ It is stretched.
   ☐ It is woven into cloth.
   ☐ It is washed.

5. In paragraph 3, the word <u>sew</u> means to make something using _____.
   ☐ scissors and paste ☐ a needle and thread
   ☐ a hammer and nails ☐ an oven

Write your answer to this question on the lines.

How are cotton and wool alike? How are they different?

_____

_____

_____

Social Science

A Visit to Hershey, Pennsylvania

Do you like chocolate? Can you imagine a town that was built for making chocolate? Well, that's Hershey, Pennsylvania.

Years ago, a man named Milton S. Hershey liked to make candy. When he was young, he dreamed of building a great chocolate factory. As he grew up, Hershey learned about making all kinds of candy. He learned how to make chocolate from cocoa.

Cocoa comes from a plant. The seeds of the plant are picked. Then, they are cooked until they turn dark brown. Next, the seeds are crushed into small pieces. These pieces are mixed with other things. Soon, they are as smooth as honey. Now, it is chocolate.

In 1897, Hershey built a big chocolate factory in his hometown in Pennsylvania. People came to work there. Hershey also built a park, a zoo, a bank, schools, and other things. He gave the streets names like "Cocoa Avenue." And he named the town Hershey.

Today, Hershey, Pennsylvania, is a fun place to visit. People see how chocolate is made in the factory. They go on rides in Hershey Park.

Milton S. Hershey lived out his dream. Now people everywhere eat his chocolates. And Hershey has the biggest chocolate factory in the world.

Content Reading

Put an X in the box (☐) beside the best answer.

1. When Milton S. Hershey was young, he dreamed of building a _____.
   - ☐ zoo
   - ☐ factory
   - ☐ park
   - ☐ town

2. The main idea of paragraph 4 is that Milton S. Hershey _____.
   - ☐ liked to make chocolate
   - ☐ wanted to be rich
   - ☐ built a whole town
   - ☐ told everyone what to do

3. You can decide from the story that people in the town _____.
   - ☐ were helped by Hershey
   - ☐ did not like chocolate
   - ☐ wanted to leave town
   - ☐ always knew how to make chocolate

4. What happens right **after** the cocoa seeds are picked?
   - ☐ They are mixed with other things.
   - ☐ They are smooth like honey.
   - ☐ They are crushed.
   - ☐ They are cooked.

5. In paragraph 3, the word **crushed** means _____.
   - ☐ pressed into tiny bits
   - ☐ thrown away
   - ☐ mixed with water
   - ☐ put into jars

Write your answer to this question on the lines.

Would you like to live in Hershey, Pennsylvania?
Tell why or why not.

_____

_____

_____

Social Science

Sally Ride, First American Woman in Space

On June 27, 1983, Sally Ride became the first American woman to go into space. But Sally's journey started long before that day. As a girl, Sally loved to look at the night sky. She used her telescope to see the stars more clearly.

Sally learned about the planets and stars in school. After she finished school, she became a scientist. One day, Sally read a story in the newspaper. It was about NASA, a group that explores space. They were looking for people who wanted to be astronauts. Sally liked the idea of being an astronaut. So she wrote to NASA. In 1978, NASA picked its new astronauts. Sally and five other women were picked. They were the first women to become astronauts.

April 1982 was a special time for Sally. She became the first American woman to go into space. The next year, Sally went up in the space shuttle Challenger. It circled Earth for 6 days. In October 1984, Sally went on another Challenger ride. This time, she was in space for 8 days.

Today, Sally teaches others about the wonders of space. She wrote a children's book about her great rides on Challenger. She also wrote other books about space.

Put an X in the box (☐) beside the best answer.

1. When Sally was a girl, she liked to _____.
   ☐ play with her friends
   ☐ pretend to be an astronaut
   ☐ look at the sky through her telescope
   ☐ teach others about space

2. The main idea of paragraph 2 is that Sally _____.
   ☐ studied hard   ☐ learned about the planets
   ☐ decided to be an astronaut   ☐ read the newspaper

3. You can decide from the story that Sally _____.
   ☐ did not learn much in space   ☐ did not want to be picked
   ☐ had a hard time learning things ☐ wanted to go up in space

4. What did Sally do next **after** her first Challenger trip?
   ☐ She became a scientist.   ☐ She went up in space again.
   ☐ She went back to school.   ☐ She wrote children's books.

5. In paragraph 1, the word **journey** means _____.
   ☐ trip   ☐ daydream
   ☐ lesson   ☐ race

• •

Write your answer to this question on the lines.

What would it be like to ride in a space shuttle?

_____

_____

_____

_____

Social Science

The Important Trips of Christopher Columbus

Christopher Columbus lived in Europe more than 500 years ago. Back then, Europeans wanted special things like jewels, silk, and pepper. These things could be found in Asia. So Europeans traded for them. They traveled to Asia and back, using ships and horses. But this took months.

Columbus loved sailing. He went on many trips and made maps of his travels. Soon, Columbus had an idea. Most people thought that the world was flat. But Columbus believed that the world was round. Columbus thought that he could reach Asia in the east by sailing west.

Columbus took his idea to the king and queen of Spain. They knew a shorter way to Asia was important. So they gave Columbus money and three ships. The ships were called the Niña, the Pinta, and the Santa Maria.

In August 1492, Columbus and his men set sail. Two months later, they found land. But it was not Asia. It was America. Only Native Americans lived here then. Columbus had found a New World. Columbus made three more trips to the New World. Each time, he brought back things from the New World to show the Europeans.

Content Reading

Put an X in the box (☐) beside the best answer.

1. The king and queen of Spain gave Columbus _____.
   ☐ pepper   ☐ ships   ☐ silk   ☐ horses

2. The main idea of paragraph 4 is that Columbus _____.
   ☐ loved to sail   ☐ sailed for months
   ☐ wanted money   ☐ found a New World

3. You can decide from the story that Spain is in _____.
   ☐ the New World   ☐ Europe
   ☐ Asia   ☐ America

4. What happened **after** Columbus landed in America?
   ☐ He visited the king and queen of Spain.
   ☐ Columbus sailed west.
   ☐ He brought things back from the New World.
   ☐ Columbus had an idea.

5. In paragraph 2, the word **idea** means a _____.
   ☐ plan of a person's travels
   ☐ way to explore new lands
   ☐ way to give something to get something
   ☐ picture or thought in a person's head

• •

Write your answer to this question on the lines.

What do you think would have happened in the New World if Columbus had not found it?

_____

_____

_____

Social Science

Early Explorers of the American West

The first Europeans in the New World mostly stayed on the East Coast. They did not know much about the lands along the Pacific Ocean.

The first white people to explore our West were probably the Spanish. In 1540, they came up from Mexico. They were led by Coronado. The Spanish were looking for gold. But they never found any.

In 1579, Sir Francis Drake sailed up the coast of California. He was on his way around the world. But his ships scared the Spanish. Before long, they built army posts throughout the West to protect their people. French and Russian fur traders did the same.

Later on, President Jefferson asked two explorers to find a new way to the Pacific Ocean. They were supposed to go by water from the Mississippi River. Meriwether Lewis and William Clark started their trip in 1804. It was very hard. Along the way, they got help from a Native American woman named Sacajawea (sah•kuh•juh•WEE•uh). Finally, in 1805, Lewis and Clark reached the Pacific Ocean. The map they made showed other Americans how big America was.

William Clark

Meriwether Lewis

Put an X in the box (☐) beside the best answer.

1. The Spanish came from Mexico to look for _____.
   ☐ Sir Francis Drake   ☐ furs   ☐ churches   ☐ gold

2. The main idea of this story is that _____.
   ☐ Coronado never found treasure
   ☐ many people explored the West
   ☐ Russians built posts
   ☐ Americans did not go West

3. The Spanish probably built army posts to _____.
   ☐ trade furs   ☐ map the land
   ☐ mark trails   ☐ keep others away

4. Which of the following happened **first**?
   ☐ Lewis and Clark explored.   ☐ Coronado came north.
   ☐ The French built posts.   ☐ Sir Francis Drake sailed.

5. In paragraph 2, the word **explore** means to _____.
   ☐ look into   ☐ run away from
   ☐ live in   ☐ build on

• •

Write your answer to this question on the lines.

What kind of things might have happened to make Lewis and Clark's trip so hard?

_____

_____

_____

_____

Social Science

How the Thanksgiving Holiday Began

The Pilgrims came to the New World from England. They landed in Plymouth, Massachusetts, in 1620. The first winter was terrible. It was very cold, and no one had enough food. Many Pilgrims got sick. Nearly half of them died.

Then, a group of Native Americans made friends with the Pilgrims. One of them was named Squanto.

A few years before, Squanto met some explorers from Europe. He learned to speak English. So when Squanto met the Pilgrims, he could talk to them. He knew a little about their life and customs.

But the Pilgrims did not know how to live in America. Squanto and his people helped them. They showed the Pilgrims the best places to catch fish. They helped them build warmer houses. And they showed them how to plant corn. When the corn was picked, Squanto showed the Pilgrim women how to cook it.

By the fall of 1621, the Pilgrims were ready to <u>harvest</u>. They invited Squanto and his people to dinner. Everyone brought food. Then, they all sat down together and ate. The Pilgrims had a lot to give thanks for. They gave special thanks for the help of Squanto and his people.

That happy time was the first Thanksgiving Day.

Put an X in the box (☐) beside the best answer.

1. The Pilgrims came to Plymouth from _____.
   ☐ America   ☐ England   ☐ France   ☐ Spain

2. The main idea of paragraph 1 is that the Pilgrims' life in America was _____.
   ☐ the same as in England   ☐ very hard
   ☐ very easy   ☐ happy and fun

3. The Pilgrims had enough to eat in 1621 probably because _____.
   ☐ they brought food from England
   ☐ Native Americans helped them
   ☐ they did not have to cook
   ☐ it was Thanksgiving time

4. What happened to the Pilgrims **last**?
   ☐ They held Thanksgiving.   ☐ They had a rough winter.
   ☐ Native Americans helped them. ☐ They planted corn.

5. In paragraph 5, the word **harvest** means to _____.
   ☐ plant seeds   ☐ cook food
   ☐ have a party   ☐ gather crops

• •

Write your answer to this question on the lines.

What do you think would have happened to the Pilgrims if Squanto and his people had not helped them?

_____

_____

_____

Social Science

Our American Flag

Did you know that every country has a different flag? The flag is a symbol of a country's land and people. It stands for what they believe in.

What does the United States flag stand for? The stars stand for the stars in the night sky. Knowing the stars helps you travel far without getting lost. The stripes stand for the rays of light that shoot from the sun. Together, they show what Americans are like. They will always be strong and never lose their way.

Even the colors on a flag have meaning. Our flag is red, white, and blue. Red means brave. White means good. Blue stands for fair. Early Americans picked these colors. They show what people hoped their new country would be.

Countries may change. So flags change, too. When the United States was new, there were only 13 states. Our first flag showed this. It had 13 stars and 13 stripes—one for each state. Some people think that Betsy Ross made this flag.

Soon, more states were added to the country. There was no more room on the flag for more stripes. But there was room for more stars. Today, the United States has 50 states, and the flag has 50 stars. The 13 stripes still **remind** Americans of how the country began.

Put an X in the box (☐) beside the best answer.

1. The 50 stars on the American flag stand for _____.
   - ☐ colors
   - ☐ states
   - ☐ countries
   - ☐ stripes

2. The main idea of this story is that the American flag has _____.
   - ☐ stripes
   - ☐ colors
   - ☐ stars
   - ☐ a meaning

3. You can decide from the story that early Americans wanted their country to be _____.
   - ☐ small
   - ☐ brave, good, and fair
   - ☐ large
   - ☐ red, white, and blue

4. What happened **first**?
   - ☐ The flag had 50 stars.
   - ☐ The flag had 50 stripes.
   - ☐ The flag had 13 stars.
   - ☐ The flag had 48 stars.

5. In paragraph 5, the word **remind** means to help someone _____.
   - ☐ remember
   - ☐ learn
   - ☐ change
   - ☐ forget

Write your answer to this question on the lines.

Why is it important for the colors and symbols on a flag to have a meaning?

_____

_____

_____

_____

Social Science

The Story of the American Buffalo

Wild buffalo once lived in great numbers on our plains. There were millions of them. When they ran across the land, the sound was like thunder.

The Native Americans who lived on the plains needed the buffalo. They ate buffalo meat. They used buffalo hides for clothing. They made tools and other things from buffalo horns and bones. Because of this, they were careful not to kill too many.

In 1850, buffalo <u>herds</u> were still huge. They could stop a train for hours while they crossed the tracks. But the trains brought white people who wanted to live on the plains. They wanted to build farms and more railroads. The buffalo got in the way.

So the white people started killing the buffalo. They killed them by the thousands. Finally, too many buffalo were killed. There were only a few hundred animals left. It seemed that they would die out.

In 1872, Yellowstone Park opened. The people who wanted to save the buffalo made laws. The laws helped keep the buffalo in the park safe. White people and Native Americans in other places did the same thing. Slowly, the buffalo herds began to grow in other parks and on Native American lands. Today, there are about 200,000 buffalo in North America.

Content Reading

Put an X in the box (☐) beside the best answer.

1. Buffalo lived _____.
   - ☐ on the plains
   - ☐ by the ocean
   - ☐ in the desert
   - ☐ in the mountains

2. The main idea of this story is that _____.
   - ☐ Native Americans ate buffalo
   - ☐ buffalo stopped trains
   - ☐ buffalo almost died out
   - ☐ buffalo were fun to hunt

3. When the white people killed buffalo, Native Americans were probably _____.
   - ☐ glad for the help
   - ☐ laughing at them
   - ☐ helping them
   - ☐ angry with them

4. What happened **after** laws to save the buffalo were passed?
   - ☐ Trains brought white people.
   - ☐ Buffalo grew into millions.
   - ☐ Buffalo lived in parks.
   - ☐ No more buffalo were left.

5. In paragraph 3, the word **herds** means _____.
   - ☐ horns   ☐ groups   ☐ tracks   ☐ hides

• •

Write your answer to this question on the lines.

Why was it important to keep the buffalo from dying out? Why is it important to keep any kind of animal from dying out?

_____

_____

_____

Social Science

47

The Railroad in the United States

As you know, Americans used to travel by horse or horse and wagon. But horses needed to be fed. They needed to rest from time to time. As our country grew, people wanted to travel farther. They wanted to cross mountains and big rivers.

Railroads were first built in the United States in the 1820s. They only ran between states in the East. Most of the train cars were pulled by horses.

In 1830, Peter Cooper built a train <u>engine</u>. It was named Tom Thumb. Tom Thumb ran on steam. Peter wanted to show people that his train engine was faster than a horse. A race was set up.

Tom Thumb raced against a train car pulled by a horse. Tom Thumb was winning until the engine slipped. Then, the horse pulled ahead and won. If nothing had happened to the engine, Tom Thumb would have won. People knew this. Soon, they wanted to build trains that were pulled by steam engines.

At the time, few people lived in the South or West. It was too hard to get there. Our government decided to help. In 1850, it began giving land to railroad companies. By 1869, the United States had a railroad from coast to coast.

Content Reading

Put an X in the box (☐) beside the best answer.

1. The first railroads were built in the _____.
   ☐ West ☐ South
   ☐ North ☐ East

2. The main idea of paragraph 4 is that steam engines _____.
   ☐ break ☐ are a better way to travel
   ☐ are slow ☐ need to rest all the time

3. Railroads were probably built to _____.
   ☐ connect different parts of the country ☐ hold train races
   ☐ help railroad companies ☐ move horses

4. What happened **after** something went wrong with Tom Thumb?
   ☐ Tom Thumb still won the race.
   ☐ People did not want to build steam engines.
   ☐ The horse needed to rest.
   ☐ The horse pulled ahead and won.

5. In paragraph 3, the word **engine** means _____.
   ☐ machine that makes things move ☐ car pulled by a horse
   ☐ driver of a train ☐ railroad track

• •

Write your answer to this question on the lines.

Why do you think people in the United States wanted to build a railroad from coast to coast?

_____

_____

_____

Social Science

Jane Addams, a Helper to All

People do different kinds of work. Some people make things, like cars or ladders. Other people have helping jobs, like teaching or fighting fires. Jane Addams was someone who helped people all her life.

Jane Addams lived about 100 years ago. Back then, the children of poor people hardly ever went to school. Instead, they worked long hours in mines and factories. So did their mothers and fathers. These people almost never had enough food or clothing. Sometimes, they did not even have a place to live.

All of this worried Jane Addams. So in 1889, she started Hull House in Chicago, Illinois. It was a place for poor families to stay. People could also go to **classes** there. Many learned enough to get better jobs. Hull House was a special place because it helped many people.

Jane helped her community in other ways, too. She started a kindergarten. It was one of the first in the country. This was an important step in helping children learn. Jane helped set up the first playground for the whole city to use. She built a hospital where sick people could get medicines and care.

Jane also worked hard to get new laws passed. Because of her, most people work only eight hours a day now. And children do not work at all.

Content Reading

Put an X in the box (☐) beside the best answer.

1. One hundred years ago, children of most poor people did not go to _____.
   ☐ work ☐ school ☐ factories ☐ movies

2. The main idea of this story is that Jane Addams _____.
   ☐ worried about money ☐ worked in factories
   ☐ helped poor people ☐ gave teachers work

3. You can decide from the story that Jane Addams _____.
   ☐ spent her life helping others
   ☐ wanted a playground near her home
   ☐ enjoyed teaching
   ☐ became rich by helping others

4. What happened **last**?
   ☐ Children worked in factories.
   ☐ Children worked in mines.
   ☐ People worked long hours.
   ☐ New work laws were passed.

5. In paragraph 3, the word **classes** means places to _____.
   ☐ eat ☐ make ladders ☐ learn ☐ fight fires

• •

Write your answer to this question on the lines.

How might your life be different if Jane Addams had not helped people?

_____

_____

_____

Social Science 51

Native American Beadwork

For hundreds of years, Native Americans have made beautiful things with beads. Some are things to wear, such as clothing and jewelry. Others are things to use, such as bags, bowls, blankets, and even tents.

Native Americans have even used beads as money. This kind of money is called wampum. It is made of many beads tied or sewn together. The more special the beads are, the more wampum it is worth.

Native American beadwork is different from tribe to tribe. The ways of working with beads are handed down from person to person. Mothers and fathers teach their daughters and sons. They show them how to choose the right beads for color and size. They show them how to join the beads together or sew them to the cloth. They show them how to make beautiful pictures with the beads.

Things made with beads are used on special days, too. At a certain age, girls and boys may be given a beadwork present. The present shows that they are now grown up.

Before two people get married, they make beadwork presents for each other. They <u>exchange</u> the presents when they marry. Their families may give them beadwork presents, too.

Put an X in the box (☐) beside the best answer.

1. Native American beadwork is _____.
   ☐ the same from tribe to tribe   ☐ used in only one way
   ☐ not very pretty   ☐ different from tribe to tribe

2. The main idea of paragraph 3 is that beadwork is _____.
   ☐ something parents do   ☐ taught to children
   ☐ easy   ☐ done by Native Americans

3. You can decide from the story that Native Americans do beadwork because _____.
   ☐ it is an important part of their lives   ☐ they have too many beads
   ☐ they are bored   ☐ they need money

4. What happens **before** a Native American girl gets married?
   ☐ She teaches her mother how to do beadwork.
   ☐ She receives a beadwork present from her mother's family.
   ☐ She makes a beadwork present for her husband-to-be.
   ☐ She gives her father a beadwork present.

5. In paragraph 5, the word **exchange** means _____.
   ☐ take back   ☐ give to each other   ☐ make   ☐ use

• •

Write your answer to this question on the lines.

Why do you think each Native American tribe has its own way of making things with beads?

_____

_____

_____

Social Science

Tania León, Maker of Music

As a little girl, all Tania León wanted to do was make music. She was born in Cuba in 1943. Tania began learning to play the piano when she was four years old. She wanted to play piano for a living when she grew up. And she wanted to travel the world.

Tania worked hard. Piano students have to learn many pieces of European music. Tania learned them all. She also learned Cuban music and instruments.

When Tania was 24, she came to the United States. Here, she learned even more. She played and wrote music. She became a very good **composer**. People asked her to write music just for them.

Tania also became a conductor. She can lead an orchestra as they play music. Not many women are conductors. Tania believes that more women should have the chance to make music this way.

Today, Tania is known for playing the piano and for being a composer. She has led orchestras around the world. She has won many honors for her work. She has taught music at famous schools such as Harvard and Yale.

Tania is living out her dream. She is traveling all over the world. And she is bringing music to people wherever she goes.

Content Reading

Put an X in the box (☐) beside the best answer.

1. When Tania was a little girl, she wanted to _____.
   ☐ dance
   ☐ sing
   ☐ play the piano
   ☐ write music

2. The main idea of paragraph 3 is that Tania _____.
   ☐ became a composer
   ☐ learned about music from Cuba
   ☐ likes being a conductor
   ☐ is always very busy

3. Tania is good at what she does because she _____.
   ☐ is from Cuba
   ☐ came to the United States
   ☐ plays the piano
   ☐ works hard

4. What happened **after** Tania began to write music?
   ☐ People asked her to write music for them.
   ☐ She moved back to Cuba.
   ☐ She gave it up.
   ☐ She took piano lessons.

5. In paragraph 3, the word **composer** means one who _____.
   ☐ plays the piano
   ☐ teaches music
   ☐ travels around the world
   ☐ writes music

• •

Write your answer to this question on the lines.

What has Tania done in her life that shows how much she wants to make music?

_____

_____

_____

Social Science

Glossary

architect (AR•kuh•tekt): a person who has the idea and draws plans for how to build a building

army post: a camp with soldiers to keep people and land safe from others

astronaut (AS•truh•naht): a person trained to fly and work in space

city: a place where many people live and work

Civil War: the war between the states in the North and the states in the South that happened between 1861 and 1865

college (KAHL•ij): a four-year school after high school

community: a group of people who live in the same place

country: all the people who live under one government and the land they live in

crop: plants that are grown to be used as food or to be sold

custom (KUS•tuhm): a way of acting that is practiced by a group of people

education (eh•juh•KAY•shun): the act of learning by going to school

factory: a building where things are made

farm: a piece of land that is used to raise crops or animals; to raise crops or animals

goods: things that are sold

government (GUH•vurn•munt): the group of people who decide what to do for a country, state, city, or other place

hieroglyph (HEYE•ruh•glif): a picture that stands for a word, sound, or idea; used as writing in ancient Egypt

invent: to make or think of for the first time

language (LANG•gwij): spoken or written words; the speech of a country or group

law: a rule made by a government for all the people in a town, state, or country

medicine (MEH•duh•sun): something that is taken to keep people from getting sick or to make them feel better

mine: a large hole dug in the ground to take out coal, gold, silver, and other things

museum (myoo•ZEE•um): a building where people can see works of art, science, or history

Content Reading